CAT
PORTRAITS

JILL & MARTIN LEMAN

VICTOR GOLLANCZ
LONDON

THE AFFECTIONATE CAT

Loves having her beautifully soft fur stroked. As soon as you sit down she is on your lap and will stay there for hours. She makes a very restful companion after a stressful day and likes nothing better than an early night. Her purring is guaranteed to send you instantly to sleep.

THE UNPREDICTABLE CAT

One moment he is quietly sleeping at your feet – the next he is climbing to the top of the bookcase. He will be in and out of the cat door one day and the next day will positively refuse to go out unless you graciously open the front door for him. He is a one-person cat as long as you obey orders.

THE ARTISTIC CAT

Eccentric and just a little temperamental –
spends most of the day staring into space in
an intelligent sort of way. Likes to
contribute to the creative process by
stretching out on a freshly typed manuscript
or dabbling in watercolours. Well practised at
posing for sketches or photographs.

THE CAPRICIOUS CAT

Impossible to find when needed as she never settles in the same place twice. She might be on top of the television if it is on, or behind the washing machine if it is off. The day you buy her favourite food in bulk is the day she switches to a different brand.

THE CONTENTED CAT

Spends hours washing and grooming and loves to be brushed. Likes nothing better than posing on a luxurious feather cushion, especially an antique one. Expert at finding warm places to sleep – hidden hot water pipes or half-open drawers. Has never been known to hurry, even at mealtimes.

THE PARTICULAR CAT

Excellent at keeping the household up to scratch – one disapproving look and cushions are plumped up, newspapers folded, tables cleared and beds made. At mealtimes finishes all his food, leaving a spotlessly clean dish. Never fails to remember his manners and always concludes proceedings with a swift wash and brush-up.

THE PEACEFUL CAT

Rather reserved, he likes to be left alone to get on with his own life. Enjoys quietness at all times and is not too keen on socializing. When guests come to dinner he will stare pointedly at the clock, start to yawn and fall asleep before coffee has been served.

THE PRUDENT CAT

Knows just how far she can go and has
rejected shredding the new curtains for
subtler forms of blackmail such as
thoughtfully eyeing the goldfish or curling
up on your best black jacket. She will never
eat all her food at one meal but saves the
tastiest morsel for later.

THE SENSITIVE CAT

Enjoys sitting quietly by the fire or on a sunny window sill. Dislikes visitors and disappears when the door bell rings. Sits reproachfully in the garden until they have gone, even if it is raining, and will only be coaxed in again with poached salmon and profuse apologies.

THE IMPETUOUS CAT

Never walks sedately, always runs. Whirls round the house pouncing on balls, spiders, feathers and shadows. Disturbs you in the night by jumping on your chest, purring loudly to make sure you are awake – then rushes away to cause havoc elsewhere.

THE GENTLE CAT

Loves flowers whether in the house or garden. Will sniff approvingly if indoor arrangements come up to standard and has been known to rearrange those that don't. Helps out in the garden by sitting on piles of leaves to stop them blowing away, keeps birds off the seed beds and does a little weeding. Can always be found in the sunniest corner of the garden.

First published in Great Britain 1994
by Victor Gollancz
A Division of the Cassell Group
Villiers House, 41/47 Strand, London WC2N 5JE

A catalogue record for this book is available
from the British Library

ISBN 0 575 05823 4

Printed in Hong Kong by Imago Publishing Ltd.